UNBREAKABLE

The Method for Creating a Lasting Love and Connection

A Guide to Communicating with Clarity, Confidence, and Heart

Shawn Breathwaite

Dedication

To every soul who has ever felt misunderstood in love.
If you are brave enough to grow beyond your old stories

and love from a higher place, this book is for you.

ACKNOWLEDGEMENTS

To my parents, as you are now:
Thank you for loving me. That love is the foundation
that gave me the confidence to write this book.

To my parents, when you were just beginning:
No regrets. Your conflict expanded my consciousness.
I will always love and be grateful for both versions of you.

To my first love, my forever love, and every love in between:
You have all been my teachers, and for that,
I am endlessly grateful.

To my brother:
You forged your way through so many challenges
so I could see more clearly. M & B, always.

To my closest friends:
Thank you for walking with me through the chapters of my
own growth. Your patience and understanding are unmatched.
You strengthen my faith in humanity.

Contents

How to Use this Book

This book is designed to help you create relationships that are loving and lasting. It is part teaching manual, part reflection guide, and part conversation between us. As you move through it, take your time.

Each chapter builds on the one before it. Early chapters teach the mindset and rules that make meaningful communication possible. Later chapters show you how to apply those tools to real moments, taking you from conflict to connection, from healing to fulfillment.

You will notice that some sections feel instructional, while others feel deeply personal. That is intentional. The Method is both practical and emotional. It asks you to use your mind and your heart together.

Here are a few ways to get the most out of it:

1. **Pause for reflection**
   At the end of certain chapters, you will find exercises or questions. Do not rush them. The insights you write down in those moments are what turn awareness into transformation.

2. **Practice before perfection**
   The goal is not to do every step flawlessly. It is to practice using the Method in real conversations, one situation at a time. If you have to refer back to the book or open it up and go step by step with your partner, do it. Progress comes from consistency, not perfection.

3. **Read with empathy for yourself first**
   Some chapters may bring up old wounds or uncomfortable realizations. That is part of growth. Be compassionate with yourself as you recognize the patterns you are ready to release.

4. **Share it with your partner only when you are ready**
   The most powerful change starts with your own
   awareness. Once you have practiced the tools yourself,
   you will be in a better place to invite your partner to
   join you in the process.
5. **Revisit chapters often**
   The Method is simple yet layered. Each time you
   return, you will understand something new about
   yourself and the way you communicate.

My advice is to read with presence, not pressure.

Let this be a conversation that reminds you that you are not broken: you are learning new ways to connect.

Introduction

The Story Behind this Book

Through a lifetime of study and experience, I have found the answer to a successful relationship. Success in relationships is not about fate or luck. It is not about finding a soulmate written in the stars, bonding over hobbies, matching movie tastes, introvert or extrovert dynamics, or even spending years in therapy. It is not guaranteed by sharing the same morals or life goals.

The cornerstone of a thriving relationship rests on one thing: the ability to solve problems as a team while making sure that both people's needs are met. That requires a very specific method of communication. By the end of this book, you will understand this method and have the tools to put it into practice.

I have little interest in lingering on the past, but I want to share briefly how this insight became clear to me and how this book came to be.

My earliest exposure to relationships came from watching my parents. They had moments that seemed loving through my childhood eyes, but my most vivid memories are of their arguments. Even then, I sensed that their conflict came from miscommunication and a lack of understanding. I remember trying to step in, hoping that if I found the right words, I could help them reconnect. Despite my efforts, I could not bridge the gap, and they divorced when I was ten.

Those experiences planted the seeds for my lifelong quest to understand communication. Why do some relationships survive while others collapse? I knew I believed in love, but I was determined to uncover what makes it last.

As I grew older, formed my own relationships, and watched those around me, that curiosity deepened. Part of me felt like I had failed my parents. Another part of me was driven by the complexity of love itself. Like most people, I experienced both the thrill of falling in love and the heartbreak that followed. The same questions kept returning. How do two people who claim to love each other end up so disconnected? Why does passion fade into distance and pain?

My first heartbreak came at nineteen. The breakup was not because we fought. Life pulled us apart. I moved across the country to pursue an opportunity in entertainment, and she stayed in school. The distance proved to be too much, and when it ended, I was devastated. Fortunately, moving to Los Angeles gave me a new focus and, unexpectedly, the next step in my education on love.

One afternoon, sitting in my new, very empty apartment, with only the hum of passing cars for company, I noticed a book in the corner. It was *Linda Goodman's Love Signs,* a gift from my mother. I had never taken astrology seriously, but as I flipped through it, I was surprised at how clearly it described the dynamics between different personalities. The compatibility breakdown for my parents struck me, and my curiosity grew when I read about my brother and his wife, who had just divorced.

Around that time, I was also looking for a way to earn money while pursuing my entertainment career. As my interest in astrology deepened, I discovered something in my chart that stayed with me: people born on my exact day, year, and time often carried a gift for emotional insight, a curiosity about the unseen, and a knack for intuitive vision.

Curious to test this out, I bought a deck of tarot cards and applied to work as a psychic reader on one of those hotlines popular in the 1990s. You may be thinking, "Oh no, this just took a turn for the worse." Stick with me. It will be worth it.

Almost instantly, I landed a brief job on the "Miss Cleo" hotline. I still laugh about it today, and it puts a smile on my face knowing that you will probably find it funny too. My role was supposed to be predicting the future, but instead, I asked callers for their birthdays (so I could apply my newfound astrological knowledge), inquired about their romantic challenges, and offered insights there. I never claimed to be psychic, but even with limited understanding, I knew I could help people with love and relationships. I enjoyed the work, but it did not last long. Once I began booking entertainment gigs, those took priority.

Although I did love working in entertainment, the gigs never took priority over my determination to break the code to lasting love. On every set, I analyzed compatibility charts, offered insights, and became the unofficial relationship advisor.

I would ask, "When is your birthday? Are you dating anyone? What is their birthday?" People leaned in every time. They wanted deeper understanding. That passion stayed with me. I devoured relationship books, layered new learning on top of real conversations, and shared it with anyone who was open.

Sixteen years of back-to-back relationships and the continued study of romance and its confusing dynamic followed. Then, in 2010, I walked away from the most chaotic and dysfunctional relationship I had ever experienced. That breakup forced a sobering truth. Despite everything I had learned, I was still struggling.

I asked myself, "If I am the go-to person for advice, why can I not create the bond I believe in, and why am I willing to accept so much dysfunction from my partner and from myself?"

Determined to answer those questions, I committed to a year of solitude. No dating. No distractions. Just work, workouts, books, meditation, tears, and self-reflection. And yes, sometimes that meant arguing out loud with exes who were not there, usually in the shower, delivering the "one last thing" I never got to say. I was always the "and by the way" guy.

For someone who had always been in a relationship of some kind, staying committed to solitude was not easy. Without a relationship to pour myself into, all I had left was the work. Who am I? Why did I make those choices? How do I become the version of myself I know is possible?

During that year, I developed the principles that form the foundation of this book. I emerged with clarity and purpose. Instead of returning fully to entertainment, I devoted myself to helping others build stronger, more conscious relationships.

This book is the culmination of decades of experience. Its purpose is to end recurring arguments and misunderstandings so that when conflict arises, both people feel seen and valued. My goal is to offer a path to deeper understanding and to equip you with tools that eliminate manipulative behaviors like gaslighting, stonewalling, projection, blame shifting, and emotional withdrawal. By the end, you will have a clear strategy to overcome challenges and build a bond that is unbreakable.

What I discovered through that year of reflection, and what became the starting point of this strategy, is that a crucial component of lasting love is a shared mindset.

Chapter 1: The Mindset Shift

Moving from 'you versus me' to 'us versus the issue,'
the perspective that transforms conflict into connection.

Despite what you may have been told by your parents, online, or by friends, you were not born a princess, a prince, a queen, or a king.

It is wonderful to love yourself and have high self-esteem, but you do not automatically earn the right to have every need met just because you exist.

Yes, you can have a fulfilling relationship built on trust, respect, and care.

But someone loving you does not mean they will naturally treat you the way you dream of being treated.

Clients often say, "I do not want to have to explain how I want to be treated. Shouldn't some things be common sense?"

My response is simple: loving yourself should be common sense too, yet we all fail at it sometimes.

If we stumble with ourselves, why would we expect someone else to do it flawlessly?

With eight billion people on the planet, it is not common knowledge how each unique person wants to be treated.

Everyone wants love and respect, but each person defines those words differently.

If the goal is genuine connection, it is worth having a conversation about what you need to feel safe, confident, and close.

Statistics vary, but many marriages end.

The reason is not traditional roles versus modern roles. Either can work.

The difference is whether both people can handle challenges together. That takes a mindset shift.

Real growth begins when you move from "you versus me" to "us versus the issue."

That shift places resolution above ego.

Most arguments replay because the original approach focuses on proving who is right rather than solving the problem.

True resolution happens when both people agree on an action that prevents a repeat or creates a plan that restores balance.

The mindset shift asks one question: how can we solve this together in a way we both feel good about?

Once you begin to see challenges through the lens of teamwork, you will need clear guidelines to keep communication respectful and productive. That is where the Four Non-negotiables come in.

CHAPTER 2: THE RULES

*The Four Non-negotiables that create emotional safety
and keep communication clean, direct, and compassionate.*

The method you are about to learn is called **Solution-oriented Communication.** It is simple in concept, but requires discipline and consistency in practice.

The first shift is moving from 'you versus me' to 'us versus the issue. Once you make that shift, you are no longer opponents, you are a team, a unit that can handle anything together.

Like any team, you need rules. Without them, the system breaks down. The method begins with one rule that sets the tone for everything that follows: **Stick to the Four Non-negotiables.**

I first heard this idea while studying with Dr. Pat Allen, who deeply influenced my understanding of communication. The Four Non-negotiables are my take on a phrase she shared with me and with thousands of others. For that, I will always be grateful.

The Four Non-negotiables
  - No Teaching
  - No Preaching
  - No Explaining
  - No Complaining

This is the baseline of Solution-oriented Communication.

No Teaching

No one wants to feel like they are in a relationship with a parent. It is not your job to teach your partner how to live better. Growth should happen in a relationship, but it happens through shared experience, not lectures.

The most powerful teaching is silent. It's done by modeling strength, patience, and emotional intelligence.

How many fights start with, "You know what you should do?", "Why did you do that?", or "Well, here is what I do when that happens?" Each phrase casts you as the parent and your partner as the child. No adult wants to feel parented. It leads to frustration and distance.

I have been guilty of this myself. Sometimes, it comes from a good place like wanting to help, to spare someone pain, or to show that you care through guidance. But I learned that even loving advice can sound like criticism when the other person is not ready to receive it. Even when advice comes from love, giving it uninvited is likely to cause disconnection.

You can still offer insight in a respectful way:
- "If you ever want help with that, I am here."
- "I have a few ideas that might help. If you would like to hear them, let me know."

This says, I respect your intelligence. I honor your independence. I am available without imposing.

If they say no, do not take it personally. That is an adult choosing their path. Give them space.

If the behavior impacts you, the Method applies, and we will get to that. For now, remember: No Teaching means letting go of the urge to instruct, and relating as equals.

No Preaching

No one wants an unrequested sermon, especially not from someone they love. Preaching often shows up as a long list of reasons why you are right.

I worked with a married couple who hit a rough patch after the husband drove home after drinking. His wife was rightfully upset. It was illegal and dangerous. This was the perfect moment to use the Method.

Instead, she reacted from raw emotion and shifted into preaching.

"I cannot believe you drove home. You have a son and a wife. You are risking everything. What if this happened? What if that happened?"

Everything she said was valid, but strong relationships are not built by stacking valid points. Preaching does not create change: it creates shutdown. The listener feels judged and cornered, even when the words come from love. Lectures carry fear, anger, and frustration. Those feelings are real, but they will not get you what you want.

No Explaining

When your partner is expressing how they feel about something you did that hurt them or raised a concern, the last thing they want to hear is a justification. Even worse is trying to explain why they should not feel the way they feel.

Here is an example. I worked with a couple who had just welcomed twins, and as you can imagine, their life was hectic. They are a beautiful couple who have very different personalities: differences that sometimes work in their favor and sometimes create challenges. This was one of those moments when the differences created a challenge.

The husband thrived in chaos (yes, some people do). He often waited until the last minute to get things done. His wife, on the other hand, felt overwhelmed by disorder. Chaos was her kryptonite. For her, taking care of responsibilities in a timely manner was not just about productivity; it was about peace of mind.

They agreed that he would complete a task by a specific date, but he missed it. When she shared her frustration, he started explaining. He thought that if she understood his perspective, her feelings would change, that by offering context, her frustration might ease.

I know how hard this one can be. Early in my own relationships, I believed that if I could just explain my side clearly enough, it would dissolve the tension. I meant well, but what I did not realize is that an explanation does not soothe emotion.

The truth is, explaining never works.

In all my years of doing this work, I have never seen someone explain their behavior and have their partner respond with, "Oh, that makes sense, I am no longer upset."

What happens instead is the opposite. The person who is hurting feels invalidated, and now they must defend their right to even feel what they feel.

That is a fast path to disconnection.

This is why, when using the Method, explaining is off the table. It turns emotional expression into debate, and debate is not resolution. It is just a tug-of-war over who is right and who is wrong.

If left unchecked, that loop can slowly erode even the strongest bond.

No Complaining

Complaining is pointing out what you do not like without taking steps to resolve it.

It often sounds like:
- "I hate it when you do that."
- "Why can you not pick this up? It is gross."
- "You are always on your phone."
- "We never do anything fun."

It is human to want to express yourself. How you express yourself matters. If it is a real issue, use the Method. If it is venting, call a friend, talk to family, or write it down.

Dumping unfiltered frustration on your partner without the intention of finding common ground breeds disconnection.

That is why complaining is off the table in a team-based relationship. Venting is natural. Unloading without purpose weakens the bond.

Anything worth addressing can be brought into the light with the Method. When you do, you strengthen your bond together.

I know this one can sneak up on all of us. I have caught myself doing it as well. A surge of emotion can easily lead to speaking from frustration instead of intention. What matters is catching it sooner and choosing connection over release.

Understanding what not to do is only half the process. The next step is learning how to put this communication style into practice.

CHAPTER 3: THE STEPS OF THE METHOD

A step-by-step process for resolving conflict with honesty, empathy, and teamwork.

Now that you understand the mindset shift and the ground rules, you are ready for the steps.

These steps are simple, but they take practice. They require presence, patience, and the willingness to pause before reacting. The reward is clarity and connection that lasts.

Step 1: Establish the Level of Importance

When something happens that unsettles you or triggers emotion, pause and ask yourself: "Is this something I truly need to address, or is it a passing feeling I can let go of?"

Letting go does not mean shelving it for later, holding quiet resentment, or storing it away as evidence for the next argument. It also does not mean playing the silent "wait and see if they notice" game.

That is not communication. That is a secret exam your partner never signed up for, and the grade it usually gives is failure.

If you realize you can genuinely release it, that is a win. The emotion passes, the connection stays intact, and you move forward together.

I know this step can feel tricky. I have been in moments where I told myself I could let something go, only to feel the irritation return hours later. That is normal.

The goal is not to pretend it does not bother you; it is to notice how it sits in your body and be honest about whether it will pass or keep tugging at you. That honesty is where real communication begins.

If you conclude it is something that will not sit right with you, that is also a win. You have just taken the first step toward real resolution. Awareness is progress. It means you are choosing to face the issue directly rather than letting it quietly eat away at your connection.

Step 2: Establish a Proposed Solution

Whoever is bothered by an issue is responsible for identifying what they need to feel resolved.

This step removes guesswork. No hidden tests. No vague expectations. Only clarity.

When you enter a conversation with a proposed solution, you make it easier for your partner to meet you in resolution. You are not only presenting a problem; you are also offering a path forward.

A proposed solution should be clear, specific, and actionable.

Example 1:
A wife was upset that she and her husband were not spending enough time together.

Between work and caring for their kids, they often found themselves exhausted and disconnected by the end of each day.

Her proposed solution was simple and direct: "Can you commit to one date night a month where we get a sitter and go out, just to have fun and be together?"

It was clear, specific, and easy to honor. It gave her something to look forward to and showed him exactly how to rebuild connection and closeness.

Example 2:

Another partner grew up in a household where saying "F you" was normal, even playful. For their partner, it felt disrespectful and unsafe.

The proposed solution was equally simple: "Can we make that phrase off-limits between us?"

What feels playful to one person can feel painful to another, and that difference deserves understanding, not judgment.

In both examples, the person who felt the issue brought the solution. That is what Step 2 is about: leading the way toward resolution instead of waiting for the other person to figure it out.

This does not end the conversation. It sets the strongest starting point: a solution, not just a complaint.

Step 3: Request Time

When an issue arises, both people need to be emotionally ready to talk. Readiness cannot be assumed; it must be agreed upon.

That is why Step 3 is about requesting time.

Instead of blurting out, "We need to talk," or diving straight into the issue, use this simple line: "I need a connecting conversation. Let me know when a good time would be."

That one sentence does three powerful things:

1. It signals that something feels off and you want to reconnect.
2. It shows respect by avoiding ambush.
3. It invites cooperation instead of defensiveness.

Agree as a couple on a turnaround time. Saying "I will let you know" and waiting a week is not fair. A good standard is within twenty-four hours. Some couples prefer sooner; others need a bit more time. What matters is mutual agreement and follow-through.

Trust me, I know this step can feel awkward at first. The first time I tried it, it felt a bit formal and unnatural. I stumbled all over my words and wanted to skip ahead to fixing the problem. But staying with it taught me that slowing down and using this step to make sure my partner feels part of the process is where connection begins.

This step protects both people from reacting in the heat of emotion. It gives space to settle, reflect, and show up as teammates instead of opponents. That is how you lay the groundwork for connection instead of conflict.

Step 4: The Conversation

When the time comes, language is everything.

We have all heard the phrase, "It is not what you say, it is how you say it." That is especially true here.

The conversation begins in a very specific way. State the behavior and how it made you feel using only feeling words. "When you [behavior], it makes me feel [feeling]."

There is a list of feeling words at the end of this book to help you identify what you are experiencing, because this part matters. Feelings are not debatable. Thoughts are.

For example:
"When you speak to me that way, it makes me feel sad."

There is no debate. No one can say, 'You do not feel sad.' That is your emotional reality.

But if you say, 'When you speak to me that way, it makes me feel like you do not care about me,' that opens the door to argument territory. 'You do not care about me' is not a feeling; it is a thought. The other person will likely respond, 'I do care about you,' and then follow with all the reasons why they do. Now you are debating instead of connecting.

That is why the person requesting the conversation opens with, "When you [behavior], it makes me feel [feeling]."

Then the listener applies **No Explaining** and responds: "You have every right to feel that way. What can I do to make you feel better?"

This response keeps the energy grounded in empathy and solution. It creates space for the proposed action you identified in Step 2: "Would you be willing to [specific action]?"

If the answer is yes, you now have an agreement and resolution.

Not everyone feels comfortable using emotional language, and that is okay. Some people do not feel strong emotions in these moments; they simply notice a behavior that does not work for them. In those cases, use this second version that still fits the Method:
"When you [behavior], that does not work for me. Is there any way you would be willing to [proposed action]?"

The listener then replies: "I understand that does not work for you," followed by either, "Yes, I can do that," or "No, I cannot." If the answer is yes, you have reached an agreement and resolution.

This style of communication removes manipulation from the relationship. No passive aggression. No emotional baiting. No power struggle.

Manipulation often shows up as long explanations, interrogations, debates about who is right, or everyone's favorite: who is more screwed up.

The Method keeps it clean:
- The issue is identified.
- Feelings are expressed.
- The solution is proposed.
- The agreement is put in place.

When both people stay in emotional honesty instead of defense, connection naturally returns.

In a world crowded with noise and distraction, clear, direct communication is not optional. It is essential.

Following these steps will resolve most disagreements, but what happens when the two of you cannot agree on a solution? That is where negotiation begins.

CHAPTER 4: THE NEGOTIATION

What to do when you cannot agree: turning opposition into cooperation and compromise into co-creation.

You might be thinking, "This all sounds great, but what happens when I propose a solution, and they say no?"

Good question. The answer is simple. You begin to negotiate.

When you share your proposed solution as a clear request and they respond, "No, I am not willing to do that," follow with: "Okay. What are you willing to do? Because the way things are right now is not working for me."

From there, you work together to create a plan you both feel good about. That part matters. You both need to feel good about it. That is what makes it a solution instead of a compromise that breeds resentment later.

A Real Example

(Names changed for privacy.)

Devin and Jaylen had been dating a few months when they hit a bump.

During a quiet night in, Jaylen received a text from an ex. Devin saw the name, watched it turn into a back-and-forth, and his energy shifted. Jaylen felt the shift and snapped, "What is your problem?"

Devin had done one-on-one work with me, so rather than react he said, "I would rather not talk about this right now. Let's schedule a session to resolve it." He booked a session for them.

In the room, I asked what happened. They offered their perspectives.

Devin: "It is inappropriate to keep in touch with an ex."
Jaylen: "Staying friends with an ex is harmless and normal."

I acknowledged both views, then said, "You both have every right to stand strong in your perspective, but let's table who is more logical, and shift into solution mode."

Because Devin was the one emotionally affected, I asked, "How does it make you feel when Jaylen texts with an ex and keeps the conversation going?"

Devin: "It makes me feel concerned and angry."

Jaylen jumped in. "Angry!? Concerned!? That is crazy. It is harmless. Do you not trust me? We are just friends. That is so insecure. Do not put your insecurity on me."

Devin: "I have never met him. I do not know his intentions. What do you two have to talk about?"

This is the moment most couples slide into debate. He explains why texting an ex is wrong. She explains why it is fine. They argue about who is right and drift farther from resolution.

I redirected. "It is natural to have questions and to want to respond, but the priority right now is the relationship. Work as a team to face the challenge. Shift from '*You vs Me*' to '*Us vs The Issue.*' The issue is the disconnect created by texting with an ex. Our job is to identify a solution."

Devin knew the Method, but not well enough to lead it, so I walked them through it.

Step 1: Establish the Level of Importance.
Devin could not let it go. So, it needed to be addressed.

Step 2: Establish a Proposed Solution.

I asked Devin, "What would you like Jaylen to do in order for you to feel better about this?"

Devin: "Stop talking to the ex."
Jaylen: "You are ridiculous."

I reminded Jaylen, "Your reaction is human, but we are staying in solution-focused language. Solutions are never found in name-calling."

I asked them both, "Are you willing to use the phrases I suggest, so we can reach resolution without distractions?" They agreed.

Devin stated the behavior and the feeling.
"When you keep texting and maintaining a friendship with your ex, it makes me feel angry and fearful."

Jaylen used the listener line.
"You have every right to feel that way. What can I do to make you feel better?"

She said it reluctantly because she did not agree with his feelings, and that is fine. The Method does not require agreement about feelings. It requires agreement about solutions. Each person gets space to process without judgment while trusting that the goal is a solution that brings them closer.

Devin made the formal request.
"Would you be willing to stop communicating with your ex?"

Jaylen: "No, I am not willing to do that."

Devin followed the Method.
"Okay. What are you willing to do? Because the way things are now is not working for me."

Jaylen started to defend. "Why? That is so stupid!" The impulse to defend is normal, but it drags you back into debate and ego protection.

I redirected. "Instead of defending your position, offer a solution you would be comfortable with."

Jaylen: "I cannot think of one."

So, we brainstormed together.

I asked Devin, "Would you feel more at ease if you met the ex and could observe the dynamic for yourself?"
He said yes.

I asked Jaylen, "Would you be open to telling your ex that you are seeing someone who feels uneasy about the relationship and that you would like all three of you to meet so he can get to know the situation?"
She said yes. "We are just friends. I am fine with that."

I guided Jaylen to frame it as a solution.
"No, I am not willing to stop speaking with him altogether, but I am willing to set up a hangout so you can meet and see the dynamic for yourself. Would that work for you?"

Devin: "Yes, I can agree to that."

Resolution. No debate. No emotional shrapnel. Two people working together to restore connection.

By the way, they are still together. And Devin now gets along well with Jaylen's ex.

I have seen this same turning point in so many couples and have lived it myself. The moment you stop defending and start listening, everything shifts.

What Negotiation Really Does

Notice how many times the instinct was to defend, explain, or argue. That is normal. It is also how conversations slide into conflict. When someone feels judged for how they feel, they defend. Where there is defense, there is attack. That is how arguments start.

Staying in solution mode lets both people participate. If Devin had not agreed to Jaylen's proposal, we would have flipped it and asked him, "What revised version of your original request would you feel okay with?" The conversation would have continued until both could say yes.

That is the power of the Method.
- No one's feelings are dismissed.
- No one is manipulated into a yes.
- You walk away feeling connected with a clear plan you both helped create.

That is how resolution becomes real.

Reaching an agreement is powerful; but keeping it is where trust is built. The next chapter explores the importance of follow-through and accountability.

CHAPTER 5: THE FOLLOW-THROUGH

*Integrity in action: how consistency builds trust
and broken agreements reveal truth.*

The next question is natural. What do you do when someone does not honor the agreement, when they do not do what they promised?

An agreement created through the Method is not a suggestion. It is a commitment. It marks a moment of clarity, vulnerability, and teamwork. When one person does not follow through, it is not small. It creates emotional debris.

Honoring an agreement is about integrity. If you say yes, it matters.

If someone does not follow through, your first step is not to react. Pause and ask yourself two things:

1. Was the agreement deliberately ignored?
2. Or did something get in the way?

I know how discouraging it can feel when someone breaks their word after promising change. I have been there too. What matters is that you respond with clarity not chaos.

People forget. Old habits return. The impact gets underestimated. That does not make it okay, but it tells you how to approach the follow-up.

If it seems unintentional, revisit the agreement calmly.

Script:

"We had an agreement, and when it was not honored, I felt [feeling]. Is this still something you want to commit to, or do we need to revisit it together?"

This keeps the focus on solutions and teamwork rather than blame or policing.

It is not always easy to tell whether a broken agreement was intentional. Asking directly can trigger defensiveness and debate. So, shift your focus from intent to consistency.

Repetition is your red flag.

If the behavior continues, you are not dealing with a slip up. You are dealing with a pattern.

When someone repeatedly breaks an agreement, they are telling you something, whether they say it out loud or not. They are unwilling or unable to co-create a relationship rooted in respect and teamwork.

Do not ignore this.

There is no method, no strategy, and no perfectly worded script that can fix what someone is unwilling to honor. This is the point where you step back and assess the health of the relationship itself.

Consistency is love in action.

The Method works. It works when both people show up and do what they say they will do. If that is not happening, you do not have a communication issue. You have a commitment issue.

Once both people begin honoring agreements consistently, the relationship enters a new phase of growth and stability. Let us look at how love naturally evolves through its stages.

CHAPTER 6: THE THREE PHASES OF A RELATIONSHIP

*Understanding the emotional evolution
from fantasy to growth to fulfillment.*

Every relationship moves through three phases: the Fantasy Phase, the Fix-It Phase, and the Fulfillment Phase.

The Fantasy Phase

The Fantasy Phase is what most people call the honeymoon period. In this stage, consciously or unconsciously, both partners bring their best selves. They highlight what they love about the other person, extend more patience, and let little things slide. There is excitement, kindness, and forgiveness.

It is a beautiful phase, and it never lasts. That is not a failure. That is reality.

Dr. Gabor Maté once said, "You always marry somebody that is going to trigger for you every unhappiness that you ever had in your childhood." After decades of study, I can confirm that this is true. Not just in marriage, but in any relationship where deep emotions are involved. Inevitably, challenges surface: which leads to the next stage.

The Fix-It Phase

This is the make-or-break point of most relationships, and where many couples fall apart.

The Fix-It Phase is when challenges arise in both partners. Romantic relationships are designed to reveal the parts of you that are still wounded, the parts that are waiting to be healed.

It is not your partner's responsibility to heal you. But relationships are the space where healing can happen. If you embrace that opportunity, this is where growth and success are found.

This is where the Method becomes essential. Without resolution, resentment grows. Each unresolved conflict leaves residue, and that residue builds into resentment, which grows into anger, frustration, and disconnection until it eventually destroys the bond.

But with resolution, something different happens. You stop having the same argument on repeat. Conflict becomes less frequent. Each time you resolve an issue, you protect the connection and strengthen trust.

If you feel worn down here, you are not alone. This is where most relationships either fracture or learn to breathe.

The Fulfilment Phase

Once you work through the major challenges, you enter the Fulfilment Phase.

Here, trust deepens. Love grows stronger as you witness each other put the relationship above egoic needs like being right, defending a point, or winning an argument.

This love is different from the Fantasy Phase. It is not based on the best version of your partner. It is based on the whole version.

You love them in their entirety. The flaws, the fears, the imperfections, alongside the endearing traits.

That does not mean problems disappear. Life will still bring challenges, but they no longer stem from old wounds or unresolved pain. Instead, you face the natural tests of life together, and that is where fulfilment lives.

But even as relationships mature, not every challenge can or should be worked through. To grow together, both partners must know where their boundaries lie.

CHAPTER 7: THE 3 DEAL-BREAKERS

Why defining your non-negotiables
protects love from confusion, chaos, and unnecessary endings.

To reach the Fulfilment Phase, you first have to make it through the Fix-It Phase. To do that, you must take what I call 'the breakup reflex' off the table.

Some people respond to relationship stress with this reflex: at the first spark of frustration, their instinct is to exit rather than to engage.

In today's social media-driven 'ick' and Red-Flag Era, breaking up is celebrated. Walking away at the first sign of difficulty is often treated as a badge of honor, proof of self-love and high standards.

I fully support self-love. I support refusing to tolerate abuse or staying with someone who consistently treats you in ways that do not work for you. I support knowing your worth and having a clear vision of what you want in a relationship.

Here is the truth: every human being is a work in progress. We all carry strengths and flaws. We all have unresolved childhood patterns. No person and no relationship is without imperfections. The key is learning to tell the difference between imperfections you can work through and true deal-breakers you cannot.

Chewing with your mouth open is not the same as being verbally abusive. If you treat every annoyance as a 'red flag' and every 'ick' as a deal-breaker, your relationships will never have the chance to grow, especially if your automatic response is to run rather than communicate.

This is why I tell my clients to identify up to (and no more than) three deal-breakers, and to treat everything else as a concern that can be addressed.

Deal-breakers are your non-negotiables. If your partner crosses one, the relationship ends. Period.

That protects you from tolerating behaviors you know are unhealthy, and it prevents you from being manipulated into cycles of drama. But if you have a long list of 'I do not wants,' you will inevitably encounter one, bolt at the first offense, and miss out on working through challenges that could actually deepen intimacy and build lasting trust.

A Client Example

I once worked with a client who had the breakup reflex. Whenever her partner said something dismissive like "That does not make any sense" or "That is stupid," she shut down and immediately wanted to end the relationship.

She had every right to feel hurt. But instead of walking away, she could have applied the Method:

Step 1: Establish the Level of Importance

She would ask herself, "Is this something I can let go of, or do I need to address it?" In this case, it clearly mattered.

Step 2: Establish a Proposed Solution

She would reflect, "What do I need in order to feel better?" Her solution might be asking him to stop using judgmental language like "stupid" when she was upset.

Step 3: Request Time

She could then approach him with, "I need a connecting conversation. Let me know when a good time would be."

Step 4: The Conversation

When they sat down, she could say, "When I am upset and you respond by calling my feelings stupid, it makes me feel angry, hurt, and alone."

Then she could make her request: "Would you be willing to avoid using the word 'stupid' or any other judgmental words when I am upset? Instead, could you work with me to find a solution?"

At that point, he has two options:

- If he says yes, the connection deepens, trust builds, and the relationship evolves.
- If he says no, she would move into negotiation instead of shutting down or running away.

Either way, she is no longer sabotaging the relationship by defaulting to avoidance. She is giving both herself and her partner the chance to see if the bond can grow.

Examples of Deal-breakers

Everyone's will look a little different, but here are some common non-negotiables people choose:

- Abuse of any kind—physical, emotional, or verbal.
- Addiction without active recovery.
- Cheating or ongoing dishonesty.
- Disrespect for core values (for example, wanting children versus not wanting them, or conflicting spiritual beliefs that are non-negotiable for you).
- Lack of integrity—consistent lying, breaking promises, or manipulation.

- Unwillingness to grow—refusing to communicate, shutting down attempts at resolution, or showing no interest in change.

The key is to pick three that reflect what you know you cannot live with. Everything else falls under 'concerns': issues that can be addressed, clarified, and potentially resolved with the Method.

Reflection Exercise: Define your 3 Deal-breakers

Take a moment now to get clear on yours. Write them down. Do not rush. This list will serve as a compass for your future relationships.

1. Think of past relationships that ended badly. Which behaviors or patterns were impossible for you to live with?
2. Reflect on your core values. What would you never compromise?
3. Narrow it down to one, two, or three. Keep them simple, clear, and firm.

Write them in a sentence:
- "I will not tolerate ________."
- "I will not tolerate ________."
- "I will not tolerate ________."

When you know your three deal-breakers, you create clarity and freedom. Instead of constantly wondering if you should stay or go, you will know exactly when it is time to walk away and when it is time to lean in and use the Method to build something deeper.

Defining deal-breakers brings clarity, but it also reveals the reality that some people resist happiness no matter what you do. Recognizing that pattern is essential to preserving your peace.

CHAPTER 8: THE EMOTIONAL BLACK HOLE

*Recognizing patterns of perpetual dissatisfaction
and knowing when effort becomes self-sacrifice.*

On the other side of the deal-breaker coin lives what I call the **Emotional Black Hole.**

The Emotional Black Hole is a personality type that, no matter how many agreements you make, or connecting conversations you have, remains perpetually unsatisfied. Just when you have done the work to honor one request, another issue arises. You meet one need, and another appears. Their default setting is discontent.

Now, to be clear, during the Fix-It Phase, there will be multiple conversations. That is normal. As the traits and patterns that were hidden or softened during the Fantasy Phase begin to surface, conflict becomes part of the growth process.

Think of it like moving into a new home or starting a new job. Once the initial excitement fades, you face the real-world challenges that must be ironed out before comfort and stability set in. That is natural.

This is why knowing your deal-breakers is crucial. If no one is crossing a true deal-breaker line, the relationship can survive the Fix-It Phase because walking away is not an option.

But if you find yourself constantly expending energy to resolve issues with someone who is never satisfied, that is a different story. It is perfectly healthy to acknowledge, "I am with someone who is perpetually unhappy, and it is not my responsibility to fix that."

This realization does not automatically mean that need to end the relationship. If you are dating and start to see this pattern, it is worth evaluating early. But if you have been married for years, the approach may require more compassion and strategy. Divorce might not be possible or even necessary, especially if both partners are willing to look at their roles in the breakdown and take responsibility for rebuilding connection.

Even someone with Emotional Black Hole tendencies can grow if they are willing to self-reflect and genuinely want to change. Growth demands awareness and accountability.

But if they are unwilling to look within, or resist responsibility, or continue to drain the relationship despite your efforts, then you are no longer in a partnership. You are in a one-sided emotional labor camp.

Here is the hard truth. If both people are not willing to do the work, you do not have a team. And if a relationship does not operate as a team, it will fail.

Once you understand how emotional exhaustion can drain connection, you can approach practical issues from a calmer, more solution-oriented mindset.

CHAPTER 9: PRACTICAL VS. EMOTIONAL CONVERSATIONS

How to communicate about logistics, plans, and responsibilities without losing connection or compassion.

Not every issue in a relationship stems from emotional discontent or unhappiness with your partner's behavior. Sometimes, it is simply about logistics, practical matters that need to be addressed so both people can stay aligned.

When a practical issue comes up, the steps of the Method remain the same; the only difference is how you frame the conversation in Step 4.

Instead of beginning with, "When you [action], it makes me feel [feeling]," you shift the focus to collaboration by saying: "I would like to discuss [topic]. Here is what I would like to do about it [share your proposed action]. Is that something you are willing to do? If not, please let me know what would work for you."

This version of Step 4 sets a clear, neutral tone. It communicates your ideal outcome ("here is what I would like to do") while inviting your partner's input. That invitation is crucial; it signals respect, encourages participation, and prevents defensiveness. The goal is not to win. It is to create a solution both people feel good about.

A Real Example

I once worked with a couple expecting their second child. Their first birth was intense, to say the least. They had planned a natural home birth, but complications forced a last-minute hospital transfer. Thankfully, everything turned out well, but the experience left lasting stress.

As the due date for their second baby approached, the mother wanted to revisit the topic: should they attempt another home birth with a midwife, or go straight to the hospital this time? She preferred a home birth but anticipated her husband's hesitation.

Because they had already practiced the Method, they decided to address it during a session together.

- Step 1 (establishing importance) was already done; this conversation mattered deeply to both.
- Step 2 (proposing a solution) was clear; she wanted a home birth with a midwife.
- Step 3 (requesting time) was handled by agreeing to discuss it in session.

Now we were ready for Step 4, the conversation itself.

She began:
"I would like to discuss this pregnancy and our plan for delivery. I have thought a lot about it, and I would really like to have the baby at home with a midwife. It is very important to me and would make me feel most comfortable. Is that something you are willing to do? If not, please let me know what you would be comfortable with."

Her husband's initial reaction was frustration. He did what most people instinctively do, he started explaining why her idea was a bad one. I asked him to pause and return to the Method.

No Explaining was especially important here. When someone begins explaining why another person's idea is wrong, it automatically triggers defensiveness. The conversation shifts from resolution to debate, from connection to ego protection.

To redirect, I asked him, "How does it make you feel when she suggests this?"

He paused and replied, "It makes me feel nervous, frustrated, and concerned for her safety and the baby's."

That answer was honest and emotionally grounded, exactly what the Method calls for.

From there, I guided him to think from a solution-oriented mindset. "If she were to have the baby at home, what actions or precautions could help you feel safer and more comfortable with that plan?"

With his energy now focused on solutions rather than objections, he responded:

"As long as we meet with doctors leading up to the birth to assess risks, and we meet the midwife together to decide on the right one, I can be open to a home birth. I would also want someone at the house to watch our first child so he does not see anything stressful if complications arise. Would that work for you?"

She agreed. The conversation ended quickly and peacefully, with both feeling heard and respected.

Why It Worked

1. They followed the Method step by step. There was no rush to defend, explain, or prove who was right. Each person took turns expressing their position calmly and clearly.
2. They stayed in solution mode. The focus remained on "What can we do that feels good for both of us?" instead of "Who is right?"

3. They respected emotional and practical needs simultaneously. Her comfort and his safety concerns both mattered, and both were honored in the final plan.

When Desires Differ Completely

Not every discussion resolves this smoothly. Sometimes, one person's proposed solution directly conflicts with the other's; for example, if he had said, "I want to have the baby in the hospital, and that is my request."

In those cases, the conversation simply takes longer. The bridge between differing desires is built through the same Method, staying out of debate, focusing on what each person needs to feel secure, and continuing to exchange proposals until both can say yes.

The Method does not promise identical preferences. It guarantees a path toward mutual understanding and respect.

The Takeaway

When you follow the steps, even practical conversations about finances, parenting, or big life decisions become opportunities to strengthen the bond. The Method ensures that both people are seen and heard while keeping the focus on teamwork.

Whether the issue is emotional or practical, the outcome is the same: a solution both people feel good about, built on clarity, respect, and collaboration.

When addressing emotions or logistics, the way you communicate matters most. The next chapter explores how to express yourself without slipping into defense.

Chapter 10: Explaining vs. Sharing

The difference between wanting to be understood and wanting to connect, and how to share without slipping into defense.

Of all the Four Non-negotiables, No Explaining is often the hardest to follow. This is because everyone wants to feel understood. When you feel understood, you feel connected.

However, it is easy to confuse the desire to be understood with the desire to be agreed with. Those desires are rooted in ego—the reason they are off the table within the Method.

At the same time, sharing what you are experiencing with your partner can be deeply connecting and healthy. Sharing is not only natural: it is necessary.

It is important to know the difference between sharing and explaining so that explaining does not quietly slip in and derail a connecting conversation.

Sharing is the act of expressing what you are going through for the purpose of connection, not correction. It is being open about your feelings or experiences without trying to persuade, justify, or defend. It says, "Here is what is real for me," not, "Here is why you should see it my way."

When and How to Share

Sharing should not happen in the middle of using the Method to resolve an emotional issue or a practical circumstance. It deserves its own moment. This keeps sharing from turning into explaining during a connecting conversation.

If there is something you would like to share, it is still important to honor your partner's space and give them the opportunity to be receptive by requesting time.

You might say: "I would love to share something with you. Let me know when you have a moment."

Follow the same turnaround time you use for a Connecting Conversation request.

There will also be times when you simply need to vent. You can say, "I need to vent. Let me know when you have a moment." However, venting is off-limits if it is about the person you are venting to. That crosses into emotional dumping. Without a solution attached, it becomes complaining, and we already know where complaining leads.

When the time arrives and the conversation begins, keep it simple. Start with, "Thank you for taking the time to hear me out." Then share what you need to share, nothing more, nothing less.

If what you want to discuss involves frustration with your partner or the relationship itself, that is not sharing. That is a conversation that belongs within the Method. Remember, sharing is about connection, not correction.

A Real Example

I work with a couple who, recently, had both been under a lot of stress in their individual lives. For one of them, that level of stress was familiar. His demanding job constantly challenged him, and he was used to operating under pressure.

His partner, however, was facing new challenges. A parent's declining health, unexpected car trouble, and other compounding issues had left him emotionally depleted. The strain began to show up in their interactions.

After reacting emotionally during a recent interaction, he realized he wanted to share what he had been carrying in hopes of finding support, connection, and understanding.

Because we had practiced this skill together, he knew how to approach it in a healthy way. After requesting time, he said: "I wanted to share that I have been feeling emotionally drained. I have started taking care of my dad, who has been ill, and my other family members have been asking more of me. I am juggling unexpected responsibilities, and because we have both been so busy, I have not had our usual connection as a source of emotional replenishment. I have felt a lot of output and not much input, and it has left me exhausted. I wanted to share this, so I do not start feeling isolated on top of everything else. Thank you for listening."

This gave his partner space to respond with compassion instead of defensiveness.

Any simple acknowledgment in that moment is productive:
"Thank you for sharing. If there is anything I can do, let me know."
Or even, "I am glad you shared that with me."

Both responses convey care without turning the moment into problem-solving or responsibility. It is an honest exchange that deepens connection. No explanations, no debate, just understanding.

The Takeaway

Sharing opens the heart. Explaining closes it.

When you share without trying to convince, you make room for empathy to grow.

At the heart of every healthy conversation and every lasting connection is love itself. But love, as we have been taught to define it, deserves a closer look.

Chapter 11: The Meaning of Love

Redefining love as conscious commitment and learning how to practice it in every relationship, starting with yourself.

According to Merriam-Webster, love is defined as "a feeling of strong or constant affection for a person," or as "attraction that includes sexual desire." It can also mean "to hold dear; cherish," "to feel a lover's passion, devotion, or tenderness," or "to like or desire actively."

We can do better than that.

As a society, we have experienced, developed, and learned enough to make the definition of something this important clearer, more conscious, and more meaningful.

If love is merely "a feeling" or "constant affection," that would suggest we have some control over it, but much of what we call love is an emotional reaction triggered by hormones and neurotransmitters. The truth is that feelings come and go. More importantly, we do not have as much control over them as we might like.

What we do control is how we respond to those feelings. But the feelings themselves arise instinctively, often unconsciously, in response to circumstances. That means that if love is defined primarily as a feeling, it sits on a shaky foundation. One that depends on how long that feeling lasts. And if we could control how long a feeling lasts, everyone would be walking around perpetually fulfilled, optimistic, and excited about life.

Without diving too far into the question of whether love is a feeling or a choice, let us make one simple distinction. When we say, "I am falling in love with you," we are describing the feeling Merriam-Webster defines: the surge of excitement and emotional chemistry that accompanies the falling stage.

But when we say, "I love you," that should mean something deeper. It should mean, "I have feelings for you deep enough that I am ready to make a conscious commitment to live as the best version of myself while prioritizing your well-being and the health of our relationship above my ego's needs."

Under the common definition, someone could consciously take an action that hurts you and still say, "But I love you," because they are referring to a feeling, not accountability. They are saying, "I have affection for you," but that feeling alone does not prevent destructive choices.

If we adopt a more evolved definition:

Love: *A person's commitment to live continually as their best self while prioritizing the well-being of their partner and the health of the relationship above egoic needs.*

Then, by definition, love becomes an active state of integrity. Someone who loves you under this definition cannot consciously take actions they know will harm you or the relationship.

When both people live by this version of love, the relationship naturally strengthens. Challenges will still arise, but each person's intention is to protect the connection, not prove a point.

Whenever I work with a couple in conflict and they come to me to resolve it through the Method, the first question I ask each of them is, "Do you love them?" I do not ask, "Are you in love with them?" because feelings fluctuate. There will be times when anger or hurt overshadows affection. You might not feel in love, but that does not mean the relationship is over. It simply means you are facing circumstances that have triggered emotional discontent.

If you still love them, that means you are willing to place the relationship's health above the ego's impulse to be right, justified, or dominant. Defining love as a conscious commitment gives you power in your relationships because it shifts you from emotional reactivity to a solution-oriented perspective.

We often hear the phrase, "You have to love yourself before you can love someone else." Under this revised definition, that statement becomes beautifully practical and deeply empowering. Loving yourself means a steadfast commitment to being the best version of you, prioritizing your own well-being and the relationship you have with life itself over your egoic impulses.

The word love has existed for thousands of years. It has been used in countless ways to mean countless things. But in relationships, clarity matters. Two people must define what love means to them, so their foundation is strong. One that can withstand life's storms, deepen through challenges, and grow richer with every triumph.

Today, when the topic of relationships arises, it is often met with frustration, cynicism, or fatigue. Many people are tired of giving their all, only to be disappointed. They fear losing freedom, tolerating another's flaws, or investing deeply only to be hurt.

But when love is understood as conscious commitment, those fears begin to dissolve. Through a new perspective and with the right tools, relationships become what they were meant to be, a space that improves your quality of life.

A relationship becomes an alliance, a partnership where two people evolve together, making each other stronger and life more fulfilling.

This is when we remember that our desire for connection is more than just a biological urge to reproduce. It is a spiritual inclination. A call toward partnership that elevates both souls.

Love, at its highest form, is a practice we live. When two people commit to growth over ego and connection over control, they create something unbreakable.

The Method is your guide to that kind of love. Use it, live it, and watch how every relationship in your life begins to transform. Starting with the one you have with yourself.

APPENDIX:
TOOLS FOR LIVING THE METHOD

THE METHOD BLUEPRINT

Your step-by-step guide back to connection when emotions rise.

Honor the Four Non-negotiables

- No Teaching
- No Preaching
- No Explaining
- No Complaining

These keep the conversation clean, respectful, and free of power struggles.

---

1. Establish the Level of Importance

Ask yourself:

"Is this something I need to address, or is it a passing feeling I can let go of?"

If it still feels heavy after reflection, it needs attention.
If it fades, release it without storing it for later.

Remember:

Letting go does not mean suppression or silence.
It is a full release that protects connection.

---

2. Establish a Proposed Solution

Before you bring the issue forward, ask yourself:

"What specific action would help me feel resolved?"

Not why you are upset, but: **"What would make this feel better?"** This creates clarity and removes guesswork.

Remember:

You are not testing your partner's intuition.
You are inviting teamwork.

---

3. Request Time

Do not begin the conversation in the heat of emotion.

Say:

"I need a connecting conversation. Let me know when a good time would be."
This allows both people to arrive grounded rather than guarded. Agree on a reasonable time frame, ideally within twenty-four hours.

Remember:

A calm tone is preparation for success.

---

4. The Conversation

Use this structure:

1. Open with:

"When you [behavior], it makes me feel [feeling]."

2. Listener responds with No Explaining:

"You have every right to feel that way. What can I do to make you feel better?"

3. Share your request:

"Would you be willing to [specific action]?"

If the other person moves into defense or debate, gently return to center with:

"I am not looking for right or wrong. I am looking for resolution."

Remember:

Use feeling words, not thoughts or accusations.
Listen fully before responding.
Address one issue at a time.

---

5. The Negotiation (if needed)

If they say no to your proposed solution, stay steady and ask:

"Okay. What are you willing to do? Because the way things are now is not working for me."

Continue calmly until you find a solution you both feel good about.

Remember:

A real solution is one both people can live with.
It is never one person's win.

---

6. The Follow-through

Once an agreement is made, honor it.

If it is broken, pause before reacting and ask:

- Was it forgotten or ignored?
- Do we need to revisit or clarify the agreement?

If the pattern repeats, the issue is no longer communication.
It is commitment.

Remember:

Integrity is love in action.

Grounding Prompts

When emotions rise, pause and remind yourself:

- **"I do not need to win. I want to understand and resolve."**
- **"Connection over control."**
- **"Pause. Breathe. Choose intention over reaction."**

FEELING WORDS
FOR HONEST EXPRESSION

Use this list compassionately, with curiosity rather than judgment.
Naming your feelings creates the foundation for connection to return.

When you say, "I feel...," follow it with a feeling word, not a judgment such as:
"You are ignoring me."
"You do not respect me."
"You do not care."

If you are not sure what you feel, begin by asking: **"Am I more hurt, angry, afraid, sad, or overwhelmed right now?"**

You do not need to memorize these words.
They are here to help you find clarity when emotions feel tangled.

Calm / Grounded / Centered

Calm • Peaceful • Relaxed • Content • Steady • Centered • Clear • Present • Safe • Secure • Settled • Balanced

Connected / Appreciated / Loved

Loved • Appreciated • Valued • Seen • Understood • Accepted • Cherished • Supported • Included • Respected • Close • Grateful

Joyful / Hopeful / Energized

Happy • Joyful • Excited • Energized • Playful • Hopeful • Inspired • Enthusiastic • Delighted • Alive • Confident • Encouraged

Curious / Open / Engaged

Curious • Interested • Open • Receptive • Engaged • Inquisitive • Willing • Flexible

Sad / Grieving / Disappointed

Sad • Disappointed • Hurt • Heavy • Lonely • Discouraged • Grieving • Heartbroken • Devastated • Low • Empty

Hurt / Rejected / Insecure

Hurt • Rejected • Unimportant • Insecure • Exposed • Vulnerable • Embarrassed • Left out • Small • Fragile

Angry / Protective / Boundary-Driven

Angry • Frustrated • Irritated • Annoyed • Resentful • Bitter • Outraged • Indignant • Defensive • Provoked • Fed up

Afraid / Anxious / Unsure

Afraid • Scared • Anxious • Worried • Uneasy • Nervous • Tense • On edge • Panicked • Alarmed • Intimidated • Powerless

Overwhelmed / Drained / Stressed

Overwhelmed • Stressed • Pressured • Exhausted • Drained • Burned out • On overload • Scattered • Frazzled • Stuck • Shook

Confused / Torn / Uncertain

Confused • Torn • Unsure • Ambivalent • Mixed • Puzzled • Unclear • Lost • Indecisive

Ashamed / Guilty / Regretful

Ashamed • Guilty • Regretful • Remorseful • Embarrassed • Self-conscious • Humiliated • Disappointed in myself

Numb / Disconnected / Shut Down

Numb • Disconnected • Detached • Shut down • Blank • Flat • Indifferent • Zoned out

---

REFLECTION AND PRACTICE EXERCISES

---

1. Define Your Deal-breakers

Take a moment to get clear on your personal non-negotiables.
Avoid making a long list. Focus on the top one, two, or three.
These protect your well-being and create clarity in relationships.

Questions to Consider

1. Which behaviors or patterns from past relationships were impossible for me to live with
2. Which values in my life are non-negotiable
3. What would I never compromise in a long-term relationship

Write Them Clearly

- "I will not tolerate ___________________."
- "I will not tolerate ___________________."
- "I will not tolerate ___________________."

Deal-breakers are boundaries rooted in self-respect and emotional safety

2. A Guided Self Check Before Using the Method

Before you begin a connecting conversation, pause and check in with yourself.
Clarity begins inside you.
This self-check helps you move out of reaction and into intention.

---

1. What am I feeling right now?

(Choose 1–3 words from the Feeling Words section.)

- _______________________________________
- _______________________________________
- _______________________________________

This step grounds you in your actual emotional state, rather than your thoughts or judgments.

---

2. Is this something I truly need to address, or is it a passing feeling I can release?

- Can I let this go fully and peacefully?
- Or will it sit in my body and create distance if I stay silent?

Circle one:
Address / Release

---

3. If I need to address it, what is the exact behavior that affected me?

(Be specific and describe the action, not the character of your partner.)

"When you..."

____

____

____

4. What is the feeling the behavior created in me?

(Use a feeling word, not a thought.)

"It made me feel…"

____

____

5. What do I need in order to feel resolved?

(This becomes your Step 2 proposed solution.)

"I would feel better if…"

____

____

____

6. Am I emotionally ready to talk right now?

Check in with your body:

- Am I breathing slowly?
- Is my chest open or tight?
- Am I grounded or activated?
- Do I feel a desire to resolve, or a desire to be right?

Circle one:

Ready / Not ready yet

If you are not steady, give yourself a moment: breathe, reflect, reconnect with your intention.

____

7. What is my intention for this conversation?

(Choose one or write your own.)

- To reconnect
- To understand
- To be understood
- To restore closeness
- To find a solution
- To protect the relationship

My intention is:

____

____

8. What energy am I bringing into this conversation?

Choose the one you want to lead with:

- Calm
- Clarity
- Openness
- Curiosity
- Compassion
- Respect

I choose to lead with:

____

____

9. What outcome would feel good for both of us?

(Not perfection — just a step toward connection.)

____

____

10. Am I ready to choose connection over control?

(Check one)

- Yes
- Not yet (pause before requesting the conversation)

Self-Check Summary

If you can answer these questions with honesty and clarity, you are ready to begin a connecting conversation.

This self-check ensures that when you speak, you speak from intention, as opposed to impulse. It also ensures that when you listen, you listen with openness instead of defense.